Stock Market Investing for Beginners: The Keys to Protecting Your Wealth and Making Big Profits In a Market Crash

By Stephen Satoshi

Contents

Financial Disclaimer:

I am not a financial advisor, this is not financial advice. This is not an investment guide nor investment advice. I am not recommending you buy any of the coins listed here. Any form of investment or trading is liable to lose you money.

Everything in this book is the author's opinion. The author makes no representations or warranties as to the accuracy or timeliness of the information contained herein.

Tax Disclaimer:

I am not a tax professional. This is not tax advice. Nor is it a substitute for tax advice. Please consult a tax professional before filing your tax return.

There is no single "best" investment to be made, in cryptocurrencies or otherwise. Anyone telling you so is deceiving you.

I am not affiliated with any coin or cryptocurrency mentioned in this book.

There is no "surefire coin" - one again, anyone telling you so is deceiving you.

With many coins, especially the smaller ones, the market is liable to the spread of misinformation.

Never invest more than you are willing to lose. Cryptocurrency is not a get rich quick scheme.

All potential earnings discussed in this book are based on optimum conditions. Actual returns may vary.

Affiliate Disclaimer:

Like cryptocurrency, I too believe in transparency and openness, and so I am disclosing that I've included certain products and links to those products on in this book that I will earn an affiliate commission for any purchases you make. Please note that I have not been given any free products, services or anything else by these companies in exchange for mentioning them in this book.

Accuracy Disclaimer:

All prices and market capitalizations are correct at the time of writing. Price and market cap information is sourced from coinmarketcap.com. All information in this eBook was derived from official sources where possible. Official sources meaning literature that is publicly available, provided by the development team for each cryptocurrency or company such as a company website or GitHub page. At the time of writing, some of the information is not available in English from official sources. In this case some of the information included in this eBook was obtained from unofficially translated whitepapers. Unofficially meaning either via computer translation, or third party human translation.

Free Bonus!

As a gift to you for downloading this book I'm offering a special bonus. It's a free, exclusive special report detailing 3 microcap coins with huge growth potential in 2018. I guarantee you won't find these discussed in any mainstream cryptocurrency forums or newsletters. These 3 were picked as a result of weeks of research on microcap cryptocurrencies.

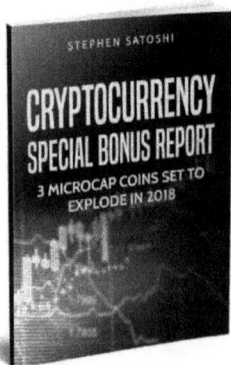

Grab the free report here!

Or go to http://bit.ly/FreeSatoshiReport

Special Offer for Audible Customers

I'm pleased to announce to my readers that I have recently entered into a partnership with Audible, and as such many of my books will be available in audio format going forward. So you can listen in the car, while working out or just while you're doing chores around the house.

Now here's the exciting part for you. If you do not currently have an Audible account, you can get any one of my books for free when you sign up (including bundles containing multiple books).

Go to https://www.audible.com/lp/freetrial to sign up and claim your free book.

And I'm going to go one step further and match this offer. So if you do sign up and select one of my books as your free book, I will give you an exclusive promo code to get another book absolutely free as well.

This applies to new sign ups only and applies to all books except my 3 book bundle *Cryptocurrency: Ultimate Beginners Guide* (although you can still choose this as your free book from Audible).

So that's 2 books entirely free! Just email me a receipt of your initial purchase at stephen@satoshibooks.com and I'll send you the promo code for your second book within 72 hours.

Thanks and happy listening,
Stephen

"Be fearful when others are greedy, and greedy when others are fearful." - Warren Buffett

Introduction

Since the end of the previous market crash in 2009, the S&P 500 is up over 290%. President Donald Trump is predicting a "middle class miracle" which will be fueled by tax cuts. It might seem like sunshine and roses out there for the stock market, and for the financial outlook of the United States.

However, those in the know, are sensing a very different financial future in America.

You see there are a growing number of signs that indicate that a horrific financial event may be on our horizon. This event isn't a something that is potentially a decade or two away either.

In fact, many experts are predicting a full scale crash within the next 3 years.

Which fortunately gives you just enough time to get your affairs in order.

You see, we've been through this before.

We had the 2008 crash fueled by the sub prime mortgage crisis, which then led to the housing market crash. We had the DOTCOM bust in the early 2000s, and the initial tech stock crash of 1990 preceded by the junk bond crash before that. These are just the major events in our lifetime. And we've not even begin to discuss the great depression of the 1930s, an incident that rocked America's economy to the very core.

What we learned from each of these horrific financial events is that a select small group of investors not only manage to weather the storm successfully, but actually come out even stronger than before.

In this book you'll learn not only how to balance your portfolio to minimize the impact of a crash, but you'll also discover the assets which thrive when traditional markets fail. In addition to learning about how to diversify your portfolio with non-traditional assets. How to legally store some of your wealth offshore. As well as further steps you can take to prepare for a financial crisis, which goes beyond mere finances and asset protection.

Because after all, this could be a game of survival.

So without further ado, let the games begin.

Stephen

What are the major indicators that tell us a downturn is coming?

I should note here at the outset that this is not a political book, and I have done my utmost to leave politics out of it. However, there are certain government acts and policies that do and will have real effects on America's financial future over the next few years, so to not mention them would be a disservice to my readers.

Many of these won't be known to you if you live in an affluent part of the country. The New Yorks, Californias and Washington DCs if you will. However, those in the heartland of America will be starting to witness these with their own eyes sooner rather than later. And what hits the heartland first, eventually spreads to the richer areas of the USA.

Wages

The average US worker hasn't experienced real wage growth in 30 years using inflation adjusted measures. In fact, there are fewer working age citizens in employment now than there were in 1975. These are the people who played a major part in Trump winning the election. Unfortunately, the President sold them short on his promise to "Make American Great Again" not by any nefarious means, but because he simply doesn't have the ability to do so, nor does he have the support in Congress to pass any of his more ambitious plans.

Trump's tax plan promised to increase take home pay for the middle class. However, study's by the bipartisan Tax Policy Center indicate that whilst the plan is a net positive for business owners, it is near worthless for employees who will see their taxes actually *increase* under the plan. This leads to increased personal and national debt. Where this is frankly terrifying is that this debt will increase *exponentially*, and exponential growth of anything is not sustainable.

Quantitative Easing

You've probably heard of quantitative easing (QE) by now. Put simply, QE is when federal banks introduce new money into the overall money supply and use this money to buy stocks and bonds. This then causes inflation, which most economists agree is necessary in small amounts in an optimal economy. The theory behind QE is is that price levels are expected to lag behind monetary inflation and thus everyone has a marginally better standard of living than before. QE is usually performed to prevent potential deflation in an economy, where people's money becomes worth more than the year before, and results in a scenario where citizens actively hoard their money without spending it. In an ideal economy, this is bad because no one is paying for goods and services.

Now how does this all relate to an impending financial crisis? Well, the Fed is currently reducing its bond holdings by $10 billion per month, a number that will rise to $50 billion per month at the end of the initiative, that's $600 billion per year less on the Fed's balance sheet. This currently decrease will lead to an increase in interest rates, and in an economy which is more reliant on debt than ever, eventually leads to the bubble bursting.

But enough with the down and gloom, what we can do is act. You can prepare your portfolio is be as "recession proof" as possible. In later chapters, I'll discuss specific assets that can protect you when traditional markets are turned on their heads. We'll also be talking about proper precautions you should take to be ready for a worst case scenario.

Housing Demand vs. Supply

This ties into our point about wages, and we saw this one come to prominence during the last market crash. A house is obviously the biggest asset that the majority of people own. So when the supply of housing begins to outstrip demand, this generally indicates that the economy is slowing down, wages aren't keeping up with house prices, and that people have less disposable income than before. This not only happened in the 2008 crash, the recessions in the 70s, 80s and 90s were all preceded by an oversupply of housing.

How to prepare for a stock market crash

One vital thing to be aware of is that a stock market crash *will* happen. It's not a matter of if, it's a matter of when. It could be next week, it could be in 3 years time, but it will happen. On average a significant market downturn occurs once a decade. The last major downturn was in 2007 and 2008, so we're right on cue for the next one.

Live within your means

No one magically starts spending beyond what they can afford. These habits creep up over time. So if you haven't got a handle on your finances, meaning you don't know exactly how much is going out and coming in each month, then this should be your first port of call.

More importantly, identify and cut back on unnecessary expenses, especially recurring monthly ones that you don't need or don't use, like magazine, newsletter or physical product subscriptions.

Minimize debt obligations

Simply put, stop financing things you don't need. Having a mortgage is one thing, but financing multiple cars when you can buy a used model for a fraction of the price, and having huge monthly credit card bills are things you can and should avoid. Owing money to multiple people doesn't get any easier in the event of a market crash.

Cash on hand

This is what you'll need for a nightmare scenario if you (God forbid) lose your job. The latest reports indicate that a staggering 69% of Americans have less than $1,000 in savings. Hopefully, this isn't you, but if it is, concentrate on banking a good proportion of your paycheck into a rainy day fund for emergencies.

Your ideal safety net should be a minimum of 1 year's worth of living expenses accessible right now. That means in nothing more than a regular savings account. You should save your money as aggressively as possible to get to this point. 2 years is even more optimal if there is a true financial crisis. You don't need anything more than 3 and at that point you're better off having your excess money in other forms

Acquire multiple streams of income

Having a solid second stream of income is a Godsend should your primary stream be taken away from you. Anything from ecommerce to real estate investments to niche market likes restoring classic cars can be a healthy extra source of cash each month. This second stream of income, no matter if it's a mere $500 a month, will be vital if you are unfortunate enough to lose your job as a result of a market downturn.

Ensure the majority of your investments have stop losses or trailing stops

We'll cover this in more detail later on in the book, but at the very least you should have stop loss orders on your major holdings. That way you limit your exposure in the event of an all out crash.

How diversified should you be?

We've come a long way since Benjamin Graham's groundbreaking book *Security Analysis* in 1934, and while the legendary investor is still right about many things he wrote in that text, his diversification strategy of 50% stocks 50% bonds is a bit outdated to say the very least.

The assessment wasn't necessarily incorrect because at the time, both stocks and bonds were overwhelmingly cheap, after all, we have to remember the book was written off the back of the 1929 crash, and there were few other assets available to consumer investors other than gold.

We've seen additional diversification since with cash and commodities being two more emerging asset classes. This led to politician and Libertarian icon Harry

Browne recommending a 25% split between cash, stocks, bonds and commodities. This included annual rebalancing based on market factors.

We can break this down even more and discuss diversification within each asset. For example with cash, should you only own domestic currency or foreign currency as well? Many analysts now recommend owning at least a few thousand dollars worth of foreign currency as an insurance against a collapse by the dollar.

Now, if you live outside the US, having a few thousand in US dollars is going to come in handy in more ways than one. I should note that due to changes in international money laundering regulations, it is now much harder to open foreign bank accounts as a US citizen, so I would recommend exchanging your money for cash bills as this will be the easiest way for you to get your hands on foreign money.

Within commodities, you have gold, silver, oil among many others. Gold and silver have traditionally held strong during financial crises, and I would always recommend owning the physical property rather than gold shares or mining contracts. Remember, tangible assets you can hold in your hand always do well when paper assets like stocks are performing badly.

There are other stores of value to think about like art or antiques, tangible assets that you can liquidate easily if needed. Real estate is another, and owning at least one house is key (remember if you're still paying for it, you don't own it - yet). There's also farmland ownership as both a beneficial tax strategy and legitimate investment vehicle. Big time investors like Jim Rogers, for example, are extremely bullish on farmland as an asset class. Then there's the opinion of Dr. Marc Faber, who recommends farmland for a somewhat different reason "when the war comes, the bombs will predominantly fall on urban areas."

Cryptocurrencies could be considered a brand new asset class all to themselves. They are a speculative one, and one with a lot of market volatility, but definitely something worth owning. Even if they make up a tiny portion of your own portfolio. Within cryptocurrency, you don't have to get too diversified if your move is purely a hedge. Owning some Bitcoin and Ethereum will do for this purpose. While we don't have any real data on how cryptos will perform during a crisis as Bitcoin has only been around as an asset since 2010, we can predict they will be negatively correlated or uncorrelated to traditional markets. Needless to say, with continued institutional involvement, cryptocurrencies have never been more legitimate as an investment vehicle and it won't be long before all the best investors portfolios will at least contain *some* cryptocurrency. We'll be doing a deep dive into cryptocurrency later on in this book.

How to save huge on blue chip stocks

One of the best ways to profit during a market crash is to utilize cash secured put options on blue chip stocks. Now if you aren't aware what options are, they are contracts that give you the right, but not the obligation to buy or sell a stock at a certain price, at a certain date.

If you don't have previous experience with options or options trading then I recommend staying away until you are more familiar but if you do, they are a useful tool to have in your arsenal during a market downturn. Essentially you make a cash offer on a stock at well below the market rate. This the equivalent of finding a beautiful property in a great location and then making a lowball offer to buy it should it ever hit the market. Your offer may never be taken up, but if it is, you've just secured a great deal on a premium property, and now you can apply this same strategy to stocks.

Now I should note at the outset that any trading with "options" in the name has a certain amount of stigma within the investing community. We are not talking about riskier naked put options here, but a more conservative investment strategy. If you believe in the long term potential of the stock, but think there will be a dip in the price in the short term, then cash secured put options are a great way to capitalize on this. Essentially you have a right, but not an obligation to buy these stocks at the lower price.

Your worst case scenario here is that you own a stock you previously wanted to own at a lower price. As these are blue chip stocks that we believe in the long term potential of, we are not assuming the traditional risk of the stock going to zero yet being obligated to buy at the higher price. However, this is still lower than the loss you would have taken if you had just purchased the stock outright at the higher price in the first place. Alternatively, the option expires worthless if the stock is still above the strike price at the date the option expires and you make a premium on the option itself in the short term.

For example, if Coca-Cola (currently trading at $43) is on your radar, you can wait until the price drops to $36 and then make an offer to buy at $33. This gives you a chance at a 25% discount from the current price and then sets you up for a strong long-term position in one of the world's most well known brands.

The one important thing to remember with cash secured puts is that you must have enough liquidity in your account to cover the entire trade. 1 option equals a minimum of 100 shares so be sure of this before you execute any trades.

Why you should consider short selling stocks

Shorting has long been a technique that the consumer level investor has overlooked and left to the "big boys" on Wall Street. For those of you unfamiliar with the term, short selling or "shorting" just refers to betting against a stock. So essentially you are betting that the stock will go *down* instead of up.

How the technical process works is that you borrow a certain number of shares from the original owner, then you sell your position the same way you would normally buy stocks, except you are selling instead of buying. At the consumer level, your brokerage platform does this automatically for you when you enter a short trade.

Some people have a moral opposition to shorting because they feel it is bad form to want a certain company's share price to go down. Really though all you are doing is spotting overvalued businesses or ones who business model is flawed in one way or another. This is how a few select investors got rich by shorting Enron in 2000. The most famous example, which is fantastically documented in the movie *The Big Short,* is Michael Burry's Scion Capital fund which began shorting the housing market in 2005 and made huge profits from the subprime mortgage crisis in the next 3 years. Burry was mocked at the time, yet his fund made investors over 400% returns in under 8 years, with his housing market bet one of the most profitable calls.

Now, I'm not suggesting you start shorting everything in sight. This would be a great way to lose money in the long term. However, shorting can be a useful hedge in terms of market turmoil, and will negate some of the losses that your portfolio will no doubt suffer.

Knowing when to short is key, and there is one pattern you should familiarize yourself with to capitalize on this opportunity. This is known as the "lower high" pattern. This is when a stock has rebounded after a dip but then peaks at a lower level than the previous peak before reversing once more. This signifies that the market is turning and we are in for a prolonged downturn.

Obviously the lower high can potentially come before a higher high, so you should set a hard stop loss above your initial short position, this is so your losses are minimal if the market does continue to rise.

If this all sounds complex, you can actually buy shorting ETFs. The two easiest ones are the ProShares Short QQQ (PSQ) which acts as an inverse of the Nasdaq 100, and the ProShares Short Financials (SEF) which acts as an inverse of the Dow Jones financial index. In other words, when these indexes go down, share prices of these ETFs go up.

For example in the 2008 crash, the PSQ was up 69% in a little over 3 months. Just a small position in this would have saved your big losses on other parts of your portfolio.

Stocks that traditionally do well during market downturns.

If you're not holding some of these, they are a great hedge when the market turns bad. Others are also solid, low risk, long term holds regardless of market conditions.

Retail

The first group of these are the giant low-cost retailers, ones that sell pretty much everything under the sun. The reason for this is demand for everyday items doesn't waver much during recessions. On top of this, those who traditionally shop at higher end retailers are hit, and therefore take their business to these lower end stores. Walmart is the big one of these, during the

2008 crisis, Walmart sales grew by 6.5% and stock prices rose 10.5% on the year, all while the S&P 500 dropped by over 30% in the same time period.

Following on from this you have the bargain basement retailers. These stores absolutely thrive when people are stretching their dollars. One such stock is Tanger Factory Outlet Centers, and their performance can be summed up in the words of CEO Steven Tanger "In good times, people love a bargain, and in tough times, people need a bargain." Outlet stores like these are also less prone to having their market share eaten away by ecommerce. If there's one area that Amazon hasn't yet penetrated, it's the deep discount market across all sectors. Consumers will still head out to their local discount store to get the cheapest toilet paper and snacks, rather than order them online.

Dollar Tree is another one stock that falls into this category and has boasted strong performance in market downturns. Discount clothing retailer Ross was yet another stock that significantly outperformed the S&P in 2008. These both could represent solid plays if you're looking to recession-proof your portfolio.

Resources

When stocks go South, resource commodities go in the other direction. Gold, silver and other mining companies thrive during bad economic periods as demand for their commodities increases. In fact, since the rise of cryptocurrencies, both the silver to gold and platinum to gold ratio are at all time lows. Both of these commodities traditionally perform very well in recessions, are tremendously undervalued at this time, and as such mining firms for these should certainly have a part in your portfolio. What's more is, the market tends to overreact to the companies themselves when you look at company valuations vs. Valuations of the commodity they are mining. Therefore a 30% increase in gold prices could see a 50% increase in the share price of mining companies.

Precious metals have always been a global hedge against currency deflation and market crashes, and it is unlikely anything will change regarding this during the next recession.

Relaxation

You're probably thinking, "what the hell is this guy talking about?, who on Earth is relaxing during a market crash?" Well then answer me this, why did Anheuser Busch InBev grow by 39.4% in 2008? They provided the cheapest mass market beer, which in turn provides self medication and a brief escape from reality from many folks who are down on their luck. No matter what the economic conditions look like, people are still going to drink.

Even though this was the year when Anheuser Busch was bought out by InBev, revenues still grew by 5% from the previous year. Then we have the big entertainment stocks like Disney and Viacom, which also tend to do well during the lean years, because people still watch TV and although they may cut back their movie spending, that tends to be more of the Mom & Dad date night movies than the family friendly ones, which still receive decent box office numbers. After all, there's no way people aren't taking their kids to see the latest Avengers or Thor movie.

We can also add adult entertainment to this. The adult industry thrives during these years, as more people spend nights in than out of the house. Unfortunately, from a social perspective, porn usage rises with unemployment. So with increased lay offs during recessions, we also see increased click rates on adult websites, and increases in share prices of many of the adult entertainment companies.

Others

As well as stocks that thrive, we have the market neutral industries such as health care, and pharmaceuticals, as well as, tax prep services and life insurance companies. No matter what the prevailing market conditions, people will always have to do certain things. These are paying their taxes, then they will get sick, and then they will die. Usually in that order, but not always. These stocks tend not to be affected by whether the economy is going up or down and often make decent long-term holds because of this.

How to use trailing stops

Trailing stops are one of the most simple, yet underutilized investment protection tools for the consumer investor. They require a little more vigilance in the initial set up stage but the pay off for having them in place can be huge. Especially in the case of a sharp market downturn.

A trailing stop is the same as a regular stop loss order, one placed to automatically sell a stock if the price dips to a certain point, except the trigger price automatically moves in line with the stock should it move higher.

Therefore, if the stock continues to increase in price, your trigger price for the stop loss increases as well. For example, if you buy Hershey at $100, and set a stop loss at $90. You can make this a $10 trailing stop and so if the stock goes up to $105, your new stop trigger price increases to $95. Then if it goes up further to $110, your new stop trigger price is $100. At this point the worst that can happen to you if that you will break even if the stock falls back to $100, any further upward moves will see your trailing stop increase further and move you into guaranteed profit territory.

If the market falls, the stop price doesn't change, and as such you have locked in any profits. This is a great way to benefit from a rising market, while still lowering your overall risk to your portfolio.

Trailing stops aren't just available for regular stocks or ETFs, many brokers also offer them on options and futures as well. These are a great instrument to have on any long-term holds, plus any new plays you may be making in the coming months.

Holding assets offshore

There is some confusion about the legality of holding assets offshore. Due to constant negative media attention, and headlines of "tax dodging" and "tax evasion". Many people falsely believe that holding any assets outside the United States is federal tax evasion and a felony, but this couldn't be further from the truth.

The crux of the law is this, as long as you declare all of your foreign held income, and pay the necessary tax on it, everything is completely fine in the eyes of the IRS. In other words, as long as you are not explicitly "hiding" income, you will have no problem with tax authorities. I should note at the outset of this part of the book, that this is not a tax evasion strategy of any kind. All methods discussed in this section are my personal opinion and not professional tax or investment advice.

Thanks to significant changes in international money laundering regulations since the last market crash, opening foreign bank accounts is now extremely difficult for US citizens. Even countries with relatively lax banking laws often hold US citizens as persona non-grata. This is because foreign banks don't want dealings with US government bodies like the IRS.

There are a number of ways around this however and it is possible and relatively simple in fact, to open gold and silver bullion accounts offshore. You can use services such as BullionVault to store precious metals in the UK, Canada and Switzerland for example. The service has no contracts so there are no penalties for early withdrawal for example. One thing I particularly like about BullionVault's service is that you can spread your investments around multiple storage facilities without paying extra to do so.

If you are going to use an offshore gold service, be sure to check that they do not use your gold as a lending device. The other thing to check is that your gold is held off the company balance sheet as an insured, allocated asset. So in other words, if the company holding your gold goes under, creditors will not be able to reclaim your personal property as part of any bankruptcy settlement on the company itself.

Holding offshore real estate is another option. Whilst many offshore deals can be tricky due to local legislation, it is worth looking into. One thing I would recommend is buying in cash if possible with offshore deals due to the sometimes less than stellar reputation of banks in these local countries. Being in contact with a good *local* attorney is vital as well, as your attorney in your home country will not be able to offer anywhere near the same level of service in foreign jurisdictions. This includes important yet often overlooked factors like setting up local corporations is necessary and deciding whether said corporation should be held in your name or in a trust. Also, buying in local currency will get you a much better deal than a marked up property valued in US dollars.

So how do you get started? The first thing to do is decide whether you have enough assets worth protecting. There's no point spending thousands of dollars on a qualified tax specialist to minimize your tax burden if said burden is not a significant amount in the first place. If your total assets (not including your primary residence) are under $100,000 then looking offshore would not be for you.

Secondly, make sure you understand everything that is going on. This doesn't mean knowing the ins and outs of the tax codes of multiple countries, but you should at least have a grasp of where your money is going, and what purpose this will serve for your benefit. This is what separates the good offshore tax planners and wealth managers from the bad. If the person you are dealing with can't explain to you in plain English exactly what is going on, then it should be considered a red flag. Lastly, stay away from one size fits all solutions that promise to "take all your money offshore so you don't have to pay taxes". This firms largely center around charging huge amounts of money to open foreign companies in your name, and then leave you at the behest of the IRS when it emerges that you are not being tax compliant. Every situation is different, and thus you should have a tailored solution for your own.

Stocks which need a growing economy to make money

There are certain stocks that only thrive during boom periods. As such, when consumers no longer have any excess funds to spend on things that aren't considered "necessities", these stocks are the ones often hit the hardest. If you have these in your portfolio, this isn't necessarily an indication to get rid of them, but their exposure should be hedged at the very least and I recommend making portfolio readjustments based on this.

Airlines

Airline stocks traditionally do terribly during recessions. Recreational air travel is something many people cut back on during the lean years. International and domestic vacations both get hit hard, as do the share prices of the major carriers. In addition, it's an industry with very high fixed costs which doesn't benefit from the recession in the slightest. It should be noted that discount carriers are less at risk as their model is always to keep prices low and make it up on the backend with extras.

It's estimated that airlines won't be hit as hard during the next recession due to industry consolidation. This has been happening ever since the deregulation of airlines in 1978 and we've gone from having over 400 carriers in the US to just 68 today with the big 4 (American, Southwest, Delta and United) making up around 70% of the market. Holding a large percentage of your portfolio in airline stocks is still not a great move though

Restaurants

Eating out is another big cut back from consumers during periods of economic downturn. The hardest hit is often the low to mid range casual dining chains that focus less on alcohol and more on food. Chains like P.F. Chang's, Red Robin are ones to watch.

Once again, the bargain chains are less prone to market conditions. So don't go dumping your McDonald's stock yet (it could be argued that McDonald's are in the real estate business and not the restaurant business as it is). Takeout businesses like Dominoes Pizza are also less affected because their convenience model is one that still holds strong during bad times.

High end luxury items

Stocks that fall under this umbrella would be ones like Apple and GoPro, those that sell technological luxury with high price tags. Although people still buy these goods during lean years, they tend to delay their purchases and therefore the balance sheets of these companies don't look as good, causing the share prices to fall. On average, people replace their phones every 2 years for example, if they delay this to 3 years, this makes a significant impact on Apple's bottom line during a recession.

Another example of this would be Nike. If Nike customers decide they can wait another 6 months for a new pair of sneakers, this sends ripples throughout the company and in turn, leads to lower share prices. Some of the larger companies may be able to mitigate some of the risk through their international operations, but the US numbers will still drag their prices down during bad periods.

Why you absolutely must buy stocks when no one else wants to

One of the biggest factors which singles out the best investors from the masses, is their willingness to go against the crowd. To be fearful when others are greedy, and more importantly, to be greedy when others are fearful.

The latter part of the above sentence allows you to make big gains for relatively little risk. This allows you to make large gains on blue chip stocks, which have little downside and goes against the conventional "wisdom" that you must make big risks in order to get big rewards.

First, let me give you an example of what I'm talking about. In 1939, a now legendary investor named John Templeton made million by directly doing against the market. For context, the market was in freefall, millions of Americans were living in abject poverty, and what's more, Hitler's Germany had just invaded Poland, the event in which began World War II.

Market fear was at an all time high. Stock prices were at 5 or even 10 year lows. Negative sentiment was everywhere. Templeton shunned this negativity and bought $10,000 worth of stocks, the equivalent of around $170,000 today. He was no stock picking genius, he just noticed that nearly every blue chip company was greatly undervalued because of underlying market sentiment. Within 4 years he had made a 300% profit.

Fast forward to the 2008 financial crisis, banks were failing left, right and center, and this was having a snowball effect on the market as a whole. Stocks were down across the board. Some as much as 50 or even 80%. Now ask yourself this. Were these companies really now worth just 20% of their value 1 year prior? Had their business models been impacted that much? For some, the answer is maybe, for the majority the answer is a flat no. There was never a better chance to buy blue chip stocks than in 2008. Starbucks, for example, rose 1900% in the next 9 years. Apple rose 966%. Ford was another that experienced huge gains over the coming decade. Once again, had these companies had their business models impacted by the financial crisis? No, everyone else was just panicking.

Let's use another example, the 2010 BP oil spill fiasco. If you don't remember this incident, it was the largest oil spill in world history. Over 4 million barrels of oil made their way into the Gulf of Mexico, causing an environmental disaster. BP wasn't even the primary operator of the rig, it was a mere part owner, but it was BP that made the headlines, and was made the scapegoat of the incident. In the 2 weeks following the incident, BP stock fell over 50%, from $59 to $27. Now ask yourself this, was BP now really worth less than half because of one incident, albeit a serious one. The answer was of course no. Investors who bought at the bottom made 80% profits in less than a year.

If everyone in a market is pessimistic, this usually represents a great time to buy. So long as the business models of this companies doesn't change. Obviously, if cars are banned tomorrow, then Ford might not be the best buy. But bad market conditions don't make for doom and gloom everywhere.

During the next market crash, many blue chip, household name stocks will lose large percentages of their value based on nothing more than overall sentiment. If you can separate market overreaction from strong fundamentals, then you will set yourself up to make massive profits when the overall mood turns positive again.

Why you should consider farmland as a hedge

In the last decade, a very interesting investing phenomena has been quietly occurring across the United States. Institutional investors have been slowly accumulating millions of acres of farmland around the country. In fact, the University of Illnois' Investment Fund now has 10% of their $1.8 billion holdings in farmland. What's even more intriguing is that these holdings have outperformed the rest of U of I's portfolio by a factor of 2. This isn't just an American phenomenon, in England, the price of farmland has risen 800% in less than 20 years. Farmland investing is not something we saw during the 2008 crisis, so it can be considered a relatively new vehicle to hedge against a potential financial crisis.

So first of all, why is this happening? The main reason is demographics, the average age of today's land-owning farmer is 58. Many of this farmers are being offered sale-leaseback deals which gives them an injection of cash before retirement. Large institutions, on the other hand, want to take advantage of rising land prices by buying as much of this land as they can, and farms represent a great way to do this.

Secondly, the worldwide population continues to increase and is expected to peak at around 9 billion people by 2050. That leaves the area of available farmland per person at a continued decline for the next 30 years. This coupled with the inevitable increased demand for food has sparked this farmland rush.

Like regular real estate, investors can increase the value of the land they own. With farmland this is actually very easy, for example, investors can turn raw land into crops or pasture or converting low end crops to high end crops if the soil permits it. There's also, of course, the option of improving the standard of the buildings or infrastructure. You can also make money from selling the water rights on your property if that is an option.

So does this mean you have to give up your comfy suburban life and become a farmer? Don't worry, you don't have to. Living a labor intensive life is not for everyone, and it takes a fair amount of financial capital to even get started. There are a number of funds that allow you to get access to farmland. Cresud Sociedad (CRESY) owns over 1.25 million acres of land across Latin America and pays dividends of 3.2%. Other options include the Market Vectors Global Agribusiness ETF and Cozan Ltd. Which is the world's largest producer of sugarcane and ethanol.

Agricultural investments are certainly not short term plays, but they can be useful long-term investments. If they are not part of your portfolio right now, then you should consider them as you move forward.

Remember this, in an economic downturn, that land is going to become extremely valuable, and even more so in an all out financial crisis. Plus, who doesn't want a farmhouse to escape to if it all out chaos breaks out?

How to hedge with cryptocurrency

Cryptocurrency not only represents a fantastic opportunity to build real wealth quickly, it also represents a useful hedge against traditional financial markets. They are a good hedge because they show zero correlation with the stock or bond market. Bitcoin, in particular, may well live up to its moniker of "digital gold" due to its fixed supply and deflationary nature.

The most common objection to cryptocurrency that many investors who are unfamiliar with it have, is that it is not "backed" by any central bank and therefore it must be worthless. However, this couldn't be further from the case and I'm going to show you why.

Blockchain Technology

The most important thing to understand with cryptocurrency is the blockchain technology that makes all of this possible. Blockchain technology allows for a permanent, incorruptible record of all transactions that have ever taken place, free from human errors or data loss.

One important thing to remember is that these transactions do not always have to be financial, they can be in the form of legal contracts, auditing consumer goods and file storage. However, in the case of cryptocurrency, these are financial transactions.

So we don't have to rely on a bank to tell us that a transfer of funds has taken place, we can see it for ourselves. This alone gives inherent confidence in how cryptos work because no single party can disrupt them. As we saw in the financial crisis of 2008, banks can and will mislead their customers and investors, a situation like this would just not be able to happen in the crypto market.

For a more in-depth look on how to profit from blockchain technology, in ways that go beyond merely investing in cryptos, check out my book *What the World's Best Blockchain Investors Know - That You Don't*

Things to be aware of when investing in cryptocurrency

First and foremost, cryptos are volatile. We've seen coins gain 100% in a few hours, 1000% in a few days and 10000% over the course of 1 year. The inverse has also happened with entire market drops of 20% or even 30% in a day. Therefore they should only make up a small percentage of your portfolio. Because of this volatility, I also do not recommend you set stop losses with cryptos, because it is very easy for them be triggered. Instead I recommend just taking smaller positions than you would normally do, this is because cryptocurrency is a true "never invest more than you can afford to lose" asset.

The second thing to be aware of is storing your cryptocurrency properly. This goes beyond storing it on an exchange, because exchanges are hosted on central servers and are therefore vulnerable to hacking. The best storage options would be a paper wallet or hardware wallet such as the Ledger Nano S. For full instructions on setting up a Bitcoin paper wallet go to.

http://bitaddress.org

Or http://bitcoinpaperwallet.com

How to buy your first cryptocurrency

It's actually much easier than you think to buy cryptocurrency. In fact, if you've ever bought anything online you can buy Bitcoin, Ethereum and Litecoin just as easily.

Coinbase

Based in the US, and currently largest currency exchange in the world by number of users, Coinbase allows its users to buy, sell and store cryptocurrency. The platform is undoubtedly the most beginner friendly exchange for anyone looking to get involved in the cryptocurrency market. Using the platform, once your ID is verified you can buy cryptocurrency within minutes using a debit or credit card. They currently allow trading of Bitcoin, Ethereum, Bitcoin Cash and Litecoin using fiat currency as a base.

Known for their stellar security procedures and insurance policies regarding stored currency. The exchange also has a fully functioning iPhone and Android app for buying and selling on the go, very useful if you are looking to trade.

If you sign up for Coinbase using this link, you will receive $10 worth of free Bitcoin after your first purchase of more than $100 worth of cryptocurrency.

http://bit.ly/10dollarbtc

Other exchanges

If you want to buy additional coins, you will have to do so by trading your Bitcoin, Ethereum or Litecoin in exchange for these other cryptocurrencies. The best exchange to do this and the one I personally recommend is Binance, which currently has over 100 different cryptocurrencies, each with Bitcoin or Ethereum trading pairs.

Once you've bought your coins you can keep them on the Coinbase website, or you can store them in a paper or hardware wallet, which I personally recommend.

The top 10 cryptocurrencies explained in 1 paragraph

These currencies were the top 10 by market capitalization at the time of writing (18th February 2018). Source: Coinmarketcap.com

Bitcoin (BTC)

The original and most well known crypto was born in 2009 and is a decentralized digital currency that functions as a peer-to-peer cashless transaction system. Each transaction is publicly verified on the blockchain. Bitcoin has the largest network effect of any cryptocurrency and is accepted for goods and services in over 170 countries.

Ethereum (ETH)

While Bitcoin can only be used as a store of value, Ethereum has many other functions. Ethereum has the ability to execute smart contracts, contracts that self-execute based on a number of factors. For example, you can set up a smart contract where John pays Susie 1 ETH if her account balance is less than 10ETH at the end of the month. Many other cryptocurrencies are built using Ethereum's network, which is what gives the crypto a lot of its value. Currently around 80% of the top 100 currencies are built using the Ethereum network.

Ripple (XRP)

Ripple focuses on lowering payments in the banking sector via the use of the Ripple network. Designed primarily for financial institutions like banks, Ripple is often referred to as "the banker's coin". Using Ripple makes cross-border payments cheaper than traditional methods like SWIFT. Utilizing lightning fast technology, Ripple can process payments is approximately 4 seconds. The currency was the biggest gainer in 2017 where the coin saw a rise of over 34000%.

Bitcoin Cash (BCH)

Formed as a result of a hard fork in Bitcoin's code in August 2017, Bitcoin Cash was born as a result of trying to fix the scaling problems the original Bitcoin faced and continues to face. Bitcoin Cash uses larger block sizes to try and reduce transaction time. The figurehead of the project is the somewhat controversial Roger Ver. As of February 2018, Bitcoin transaction fees were lower than Bitcoin Cash for the first time ever.

Litecoin (LTC)

Litecoin has been dubbed the "silver" to Bitcoin's "gold". Like Bitcoin, it's purely a method of transaction. However, it's a faster, more lightweight currency that processes transactions 4 times faster than the Bitcoin network and with lower fees. Litecoin benefits from being the lowest priced coin on Coinbase which is most user's first entry into the cryptocurrency market.

Cardano (ADA)

An ambitious cryptocurrency project with a team of academics behind it. Cardano essentially aims to solve all the problems that other major coins face. They use a proof-of-stake mining system which is more energy efficient than proof-of-work used by Bitcoin. The one drawback for Cardano right now is that there is no working product, so their technology is still largely in the theoretical stages. Some have sarcastically named it the "$16 billion whitepaper" due to the lack of product and high market cap.

Neo (NEO)

Dubbed "the Ethereum of China", Neo was one of the biggest crypto success stories in 2017. It too can run smart contracts and decentralized applications on the platform. Neo's access to the Chinese market can it a huge advantage when it comes to other cryptocurrencies. China has had a tumultuous relationship with cryptos and Neo having its home base there may be hugely beneficial going forward.

Stellar (XLM)

Stellar is another coin that focuses on payment processing. With a particular target on the third world, and underbanked countries rather than banks and other financial institutions. The project received a lot of attention in late 2017 and received funding from IBM. You can think of Stellar as a more decentralized version of Ripple.

EOS (EOS)

A decentralized infrastructure to run applications. Kind of like a programming language or video game engine that is reusable for different purposes. EOS is very excited for programmers and the eventual aim is to make it accessible to regular folks as well. The goal is to make decentralized apps mainstream, so normal users can benefit from them without even needing to understand how blockchain technology works.

Dash (DASH)

Rounding out the top 10 we have Dash, short for Digital Cash. Another coin focused on payment transactions, but with a twist. Dash can be used anonymously using its DarkSend protocol. There are also significant passive income opportunities that can be had by hosting a Masternode, which keeps the Dash ecosystem running. However, at the time of writing one of these nodes works out at about $60,000.

For more information on cryptocurrency along with a fundamental analysis of 12 different coins, check out my bestselling primer to the subject *Cryptocurrency: Beginners Bible*

What part should crypto play in your portfolio?

I recommend cryptocurrency make up no more than 20% of your overall portfolio, and this number should decrease as you get closer to retirement age. For example, if you are 65 or older, crypto should make up no more than 10% of your overall holdings.

I believe everyone should hold Bitcoin as part of their crypto holdings and there are a few reasons for this. The first of which is that currently, the entire market is loosely tied to the performance of Bitcoin itself. If

Bitcoin is performing badly, the media headlines are focused on this and money goes out of the market. Conversely, when Bitcoin is performing well, this is what leads new money to flood into the market, as we saw in November and December of 2017 when Coinbase became the most downloaded app on the app store. The other coins tend to grow when Bitcoin's price is stagnant.

I believe in holding some Ethereum as well, because 80 of the top 100 coins by market cap are built on the Ethereum platform. You could also hedge this with some Neo if you wanted to bet big on China. There are also coins which focus on the supply chain management sector, in which blockchain technology will see its first widespread adoption cases. The main ones of these are VeChain, WaltonChain and Modum, with smaller projects like Ambrosus also worth investigating.

Are there any cryptocurrencies I recommend you avoid? The only ones I would lump in this category would be any coin that seemingly operates a pyramid scheme or guaranteed returns investment program. I previously warned readers about BitConnect and DavorCoin before both of these operations pulled exit scams causing prices to fall by over 95%. FalconCoin is another one that falls into this category and you should stay well away from.

I do recommend researching any coin you plan on investing in. Going in blind with the hope of quick huge returns is an easy way to lose money in this market. Coins with legitimate use cases and long term potential should be where your money goes.

Why you should have a grab bag ready

In a worst case scenario situation, when you need to leave home immediately, you absolutely must be prepared. This could be anything from a natural disaster like an Earthquake or Hurricane. To a terrorist attack on your neighborhood. Or even attacks by local militias in the case of a civil war. While all these scenarios are unlikely to happen to you personally, this is an insurance type situation. Hopefully, you will never need it, but if and when you do, you'll be glad you have it.

This means having a bag ready to go by the front door that you can literally grab and go at a moment's notice. The bag itself should be small, no larger than an overnight sized backpack (55L), preferably even smaller than that (around 40L). You don't want to be weighed down by its contents either. Here are 11 things this bag must contain.

1.   Identification

In the case of police checkpoints, checking in hotels and motels, you will need some form of government ID. You should also keep photocopies of these as well. This applies to all members of your family

2.   Cash

You'll need emergency cash in case the ATM network is affected like in the case of a cyber attack. Remember, cash is king in these kinds of situations. I recommend having at least 1 week's worth of cash, stored in different compartments in the bag. There are additional ways to keep it safe in the case of concealable belts and bras so consider spending $20 and having one of these.

3.   Medicine and first aid materials

If you or your family take prescription medication, have an extra bottle or supply in your bag. Remember many prescription drugs lose effectiveness after 2 or 3 years so be sure to replace this regularly. In addition a small first aid kit with band aids, antiseptic ointment etc. Can be very handy in a disaster scenario. Keep an epi-pen around as well, even if no one in your family is diabetic.

4.   Contact details of friends and family

Chances are your cellphone will be on your person, but if the battery goes dead, you should have hard copy addresses and phone numbers of your immediate family so you can get in touch with them if need be. Remember, pay phones are still in existence.

5. Swiss army knife and other multi-tool

You'll need a can opener for food, screwdrivers and knives for miscellaneous tasks. A Swiss army knife is a life saver in these kinds of situations. Pro tip: Get one with a torch on to save you having to carry a separate torch.

6. Food and water

This is space permitting but you should ideally have at least 24 hours worth of food and water in the bag. You can buy canned goods and meal pouches with a 25 year shelf life from supply stores like wisefoodstorage.com

Regarding water, this is a tricky one as ideally you want 1.5L per person per day, and that amount adds both a lot of weight and a lot of space. As an alternative, you can buy bottles with built-in filtration systems that remove the need for bottled water. These can be used with any water source you come across. You can also use water purification tablets for this purpose.

7. Basic hygiene provisions

Toothbrushes, toothpaste, some deodorant, toilet paper, disinfectant alcohol spray like Purell, and wet wipes. Just the bare necessities to make the next day or two slightly more bearable if you end up being stuck without a shower.

8. Local area map

If your phone dies or the GPS stops working, you'll need to go old school. So if you don't know how to read one, probably best learn now.

9. Cold weather clothes

Remember, if it's hot you can always take clothes off, but if it's cold you'll need something on top. One thick sweater for each family member should suffice, perhaps a wooly hat each if you have space because we lose most of our body heat through our heads.

10. Mini AM/FM radio - preferably with shortwave capability

If all cell towers are down, the radio network will be your best way to keep informed of what's going on. Find out the emergency radio frequencies and have them written down. Ensure you radio is a wind up model as well so you don't have to rely on an external power source.

11. Whistle

This might be your most important tool of all. If you immediately need to get people's attention in an emergency, then this will be your best friend.

I should also note that due to the controversial nature of the topic, I have deliberately not discussed firearms in this section.

The New Economy and Barter items

In the case of a total financial collapse, the way we look at money is going to be turned on its head. This could be as a result of hyperinflation like we saw in Zimbabwe and more recently in Venezuela.

For the initial period, we'll be no longer relying on our platinum cards to take care of day to day transactions. We'll be going old school instead. Cash will be very much king, but we should also discuss barter items as well.

Physical Gold & Silver

Not the paper gold your might buy in an ETF. I'm talking real, tangible gold and silver that you can hold in your hands and see with your own eyes. Gold has had intrinsic value for hundreds and years, and the same goes for its younger brother silver. In the event that a government introduces a new fiat currency, for example, these metals will hold their value.

This doesn't just include physical bars and coins. This can be in the form of jewelry as well.

Stores of Value

We've already discussed gold and silver, but there are other physical stores of value that would hold up well against a currency collapse. For example watches, jewelry, art and real estate all have inherent worth in their physical form. Obviously, it's easier to liquidate a watch than it is an entire home, but both will perform well even if the is a dire fiat currency situation ongoing.

Cryptocurrency

If you're unfamiliar with cryptocurrency then this might seem like a strange pick. However, we've already seen this in action in cases like Venezuela, where many citizens turned to Bitcoin in an attempt to negate the crippling effects of the country's hyperinflation. For example, the case of engineer John Villar who purchased vital medical supplies online using Bitcoin to help treat his sick wife. This was after stifling shortages within the country's own health service.

Bitcoin and other cryptocurrencies can be transacted merely by scanning a code on a smartphone, with the receiver getting the funds within a matter of minutes or even seconds. This makes them far more liquid and fungible than other items such as gold for example. You can also spend fractions of cryptocurrencies without difficulty. So this could well be a new way of bartering that we see during the next financial crisis.

Day to Day Bartering Items

Medical Supplies

Arguably the most vital of the short-term bartering goods is medical supplies. Nothing becomes more necessary in a short space of time than things like insulin, antibiotics, blood thinners and painkillers. Lower on the spectrum you have non-emergency items like antiseptic, rubbing alcohol and iodine. Even beyond bartering, having these on hand may well make you a hero to someone else during a crisis, and that alone is why they are well worth keeping around.

Salt

Salt has been long used as a barter item for over two thousand years, dating all the way back to Roman times. Not only is it a vital mineral for our bodies, it's also the number one key ingredient in cooking and preserving food. Stored in an airtight container, salt can last for decades so I would recommend having a few kilos in the house for both personal use and as a potential bartering opportunity.

Batteries

An item that's relatively light and you can keep a lot of around but one that proves invaluable in a disaster scenario. People need batteries to power flashlights, radios and walkie talkies, so having some spares on hand is going to make you very popular indeed.

Gasoline

It might seem abundant now, but what many of you may not know is that gas was actually rationed during World War II. People were only allowed 3 gallons per week, and it sent "black gold" prices soaring. Keeping a few spare gallons will be of huge benefit to you during a worst case scenario type situation as people require fuel for their vehicles as well as if they are running any generators to power their homes. If you really want to go all out you can learn to make your own biodiesel.

Conclusion

Hopefully this book has given you a better understanding of how you can protect your portfolio, your wealth and your family in the case of a significant downturn, or even an all out crash. And in some cases, how you can even come out ahead when the market turns bullish again.

By diversifying your assets, and incorporating some alternative investments into your portfolio, you can hedge against any losses your traditional investments may incur when the market turns bearish. From farmland to rare metals, to cryptocurrency, adding these to your portfolio can massively negate any losses your stocks or bonds may incur.

We've also discussed potential "worst case scenario" type options and how you can adequately prepare yourself for these. We pray that these are just hypothetical, but these are the types of situations that if you don't plan your strategy in advance, you will wish you had. Having a go bag ready by the door containing all your essential items will be something your family thanks you for if anything does go down that requires you to need it.

I hope you've enjoyed this book, and that you've learned some new things after reading it that you can apply to your own asset protection strategy. If you have then I'd really appreciate it if you left a review on Amazon.

I wish you the very best for your financial future,
Stephen Satoshi

P.S. One of the best hedging options I've mentioned in this book is cryptocurrency. If you haven't yet bought any crypto then the easiest way to do so is to use Coinbase. If you sign up using this link and buy more than $100 worth of Bitcoin, Ethereum or Litecoin then you will receive a $10 bonus.

http://bit.ly/10dollarbtc

Other Books by Stephen Satoshi

All books available on Amazon with audio versions available on Audible where possible.

Cryptocurrency: Beginners Bible (also available in audio)

Blockchain: Beginners Bible (also available in audio)

Bitcoin: Beginners Bible (also available in audio)

Cryptocurrency: The Ultimate Beginners Guide (contains the 3 above books at a discounted rate - also available in audio)

Cryptocurrency: Insider Secrets - 12 Exclusive Coins Under $1 with Huge Growth Potential in 2018

Ethereum: Beginners Bible (also available in audio)

Cryptocurrency: Top 10 Trading Mistakes Newbies Make - And How To Avoid Them (also available in audio)

Cryptocurrency: 13 More Coins to Watch with 10X Growth Potential in 2018 (also available in audio)

Cryptocurrency 3.0 - Ultra Fast, Zero Transaction Fee, Futureproof Coins That Need to be on Your Radar (also available in audio)

Cryptocurrency: What The World's Best Blockchain Investors Know - That You Don't

Stock Investing for Beginners: Marijuana Stocks - How to Get Rich With The Only Asset Producing Financial Returns as Fast as Cryptocurrency

Future books:

If there are any specific cryptocurrencies or cryptocurrency related topics you would like to see covered in future books then you can email me at Stephen@satoshibooks.com and I'll do my best to cover them in new releases

www.ingramcontent.com/pod-product-compliance
Lightning Source LLC
Chambersburg PA
CBHW071501210326
41597CB00018B/2644